SCHOLASTIC

WRITING PRACTICE

D1608686

New York • Toronto • London • Auckland • Sydney
Mexico City • New Delhi • Hong Kong • Buenos Aires

Teaching *Resources*

Cover design by Jay Namerow
Interior illustrations by Kathy Marlin
Interior design by Quack & Company

ISBN 0-439-81913-X

4 5 6 7 8 9 10 08 13 12 11

Table of Contents

Dear Parent:

Welcome to *4th Grade Writing Practice!* This valuable tool is designed to help your child succeed in school. Scholastic, the most trusted name in learning, has been creating quality educational materials for school and home for nearly a century. And this resource is no exception.

Inside this book, you'll find colorful and engaging activity pages that will give your child the practice he or she needs to master essential skills, such as writing complete sentences, identifying parts of sentences, writing paragraphs, proofreading, and so much more.

To support your child's learning experience at home, try these helpful tips:

- Provide a comfortable, well-lit place to work, making sure your child has all the supplies he or she needs.

- Encourage your child to work at his or her own pace. Children learn at different rates and will naturally develop skills in their own time.

- Praise your child's efforts. If your child makes a mistake, offer words of encouragement and positive help.

- Display your child's work and celebrate his successes with family and friends.

We hope you and your child will enjoy working together to complete this workbook.

Happy learning!
The Editors

Sassy Sentences

*A **sentence** is a group of words that expresses a complete thought. When you write a sentence, you put your thoughts into words. If the sentence is complete, the meaning is clear. It contains a subject (the naming part) and a predicate (an action or state of being part).*

These are sentences.
Sally sells seashells at the seashore.
Betty Botter bought a bit of better butter.

These are not sentences.
Peck of pickled peppers.
Flying up a flue.

Make complete sentences by adding words to each group of words. Try to create tongue twisters like the sentences above.

1. _____ flips fine flapjacks.

2. Sixty slippery seals _____.

3. _____ fed Ted _____.

4. Ruby Rugby's baby brother _____.

5. _____ managing an imaginary magazine.

6. Sam's sandwich shop _____.

7. _____ back blue balloons.

8. _____ pink peacock pompously _____.

9. Pete's pop Pete _____.

10. _____ sawed Mr. Saw's _____.

11. A flea and a fly _____.

12. _____ black-backed bumblebee.

Create your own tongue twisters to share with friends. Make sure each one expresses a complete thought.

Link It Together

A sentence needs two parts, a subject and a predicate, to express a complete thought.
The **subject part** tells whom or what the sentence is about.
The **predicate part** tells what the subject is or does.

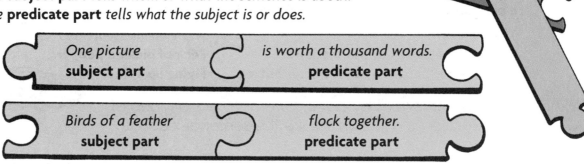

One picture	is worth a thousand words.
subject part	**predicate part**

Birds of a feather	flock together.
subject part	**predicate part**

A. Read the subject and predicate parts from some other famous sayings. Write *S* next to each subject part. Write *P* next to each predicate part.

_____ half a loaf   _____ must go on

_____ one good turn   _____ gathers no moss

_____ spoils the whole barrel   _____ has a silver lining

_____ the show   _____ makes waste

_____ every cloud   _____ one rotten apple

_____ deserves another   _____ a rolling stone

_____ catches the worm   _____ is better than none

_____ the early bird   _____ haste

B. Now combine the subject and predicate parts to create these famous sayings.

1. _____

2. _____

3. _____

4. _____

5. _____

6. _____

7. _____

8. _____

Make up some sayings of your own. Then circle the subject part and underline the predicate part of each sentence.

Scholastic Teaching Resources

That's Groovy!

There are four kinds of sentences. Each one does something different.

A **declarative sentence** tells something.
It is a **statement** and ends with a period.

My grandparents grew up during the 1960s.

An **interrogative sentence** asks something.
It is a **question** and ends with a question mark.

Do you know who the hippies were?

An **imperative sentence** tells someone to do something.
It is a **command** and ends with a period.

Check out this photo of my grandmother.

An **exclamatory sentence** shows strong feeling.
It is an **exclamation** and ends with an exclamation point.

Now that's one strange-looking outfit she has on!

Read the following sentences. Identify what kind of sentence each one is. Write *S* for statement, *Q* for question, *C* for command, and *E* for exclamation.

_____ **1.** Grandma says there was a fashion revolution in the 1960s.

_____ **2.** What an amazing time it must have been!

_____ **3.** Here's a photo of my grandfather in his teens.

_____ **4.** How do you like those sideburns and the long hair?

_____ **5.** Take a look at what he's wearing.

_____ **6.** I don't believe those bellbottoms and sandals!

_____ **7.** Please tell me he's not wearing beads.

_____ **8.** I'm glad these fashions are no longer in style!

_____ **9.** Have you ever seen anything so funny?

_____ **10.** Try not to laugh too hard.

_____ **11.** One day our grandchildren may laugh at us.

_____ **12.** What's so funny about what we're wearing?

A Whale of a Fish

When you write, the words and phrases in your sentences must be in an order that makes sense. Compare the sentences in each pair. Which ones make more sense?

An enormous fish what the whale shark is!
What an enormous fish the whale shark is!

The largest fish in the world the whale shark is.
The whale shark is the largest fish in the world.

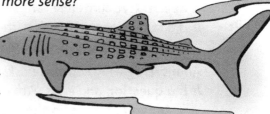

Use each group of words to write a sentence that makes sense.

1. of 60 feet?   that the whale shark   Did you know   to a length   can grow

_____

2. two school buses   end to end!   That's about   parked   as long as

_____

3. are not a threat   These huge creatures   like some other sharks are.   to humans

_____

4. to look for   float near the surface   plankton and tiny fish.   Whale sharks

_____

5. it must be   alongside a whale shark.   Imagine   to swim   how amazing

_____

Now rewrite the following sentences so that the words and phrases are in an order that makes better sense.

6. An estimated 20,000 known species of fish there are in the world.

_____

7. Of all these species the smallest is the dwarf pygmy goby?

_____

8. When it is fully grown is less than a half-inch long this species of goby!

_____

9. In the massive Indian Ocean makes its home this tiny fish.

_____

Scholastic Teaching Resources

Number Sentences

 *Words such as **who**, **what**, **where**, **why**, **when**, and **how**, and helping verbs such as **is**, **are**, **was**, **were**, **do**, **did**, and **can** at the beginning of sentences, signal interrogative sentences or questions.*

> **What** *is an odd number?*
> **Do** *you know what an even number is?*
> **Is** *2 an odd number or an even number?*

Change each statement below into a question. Remember to begin and end each sentence correctly.

1. Numbers that cannot be divided evenly by 2 are called odd numbers.

_____

2. All even numbers can be divided evenly by 2.

_____

3. Zero is considered an even number.

_____

4. Numbers that have 0, 2, 4, 6, or 8 in the ones place are even numbers.

_____

5. Odd numbers end in 1, 3, 5, 7, or 9.

_____

6. The number 317,592 is an even number because it ends in 2.

_____

7. The sum is always an even number when you add two even numbers.

_____

8. The sum of two odd numbers is also an even number.

_____

9. The same rule applies if you subtract an odd number from an odd number.

_____

10. You can figure out all the rules for working with odd and even numbers.

_____

Proofing Pays

Capitalization and end punctuation help show where one sentence ends and the next one begins. Whenever you write, proofread to make sure each sentence begins with a capital letter and ends correctly. Here's an example of how to mark the letters that should be capitalized.

h̲ave you ever heard of a Goliath birdeater? i̲t is
the world's largest spider. t̲his giant tarantula can grow
to 11 inches in length and weigh about 6 ounces. n̲ow that's
a big spider! a̲lthough it is called a birdeater, it usually
eats small reptiles and insects. t̲hese spiders are
mostly found in rain forests.

Read the passage below. It is about another amazing animal, but it is not so easy to read because the writer forgot to add end punctuation and to use capital letters at the beginning of sentences. Proofread the passage. Mark the letters that should be capitals with the capital letter symbol. Put the correct punctuation marks at the ends of sentences. Then reread the passage.

think about the fastest car you've ever seen in the Indianapolis 500 race

that's about how fast a peregrine falcon dives it actually reaches speeds up to

175 miles an hour how incredibly fast they are peregrine falcons are also very

powerful birds did you know that they can catch and kill their prey in the air

using their sharp claws what's really amazing is that peregrine falcons live in

both the country and in the city keep on the lookout if you're ever in New York

City believe it or not, it is home to a very large population of falcons

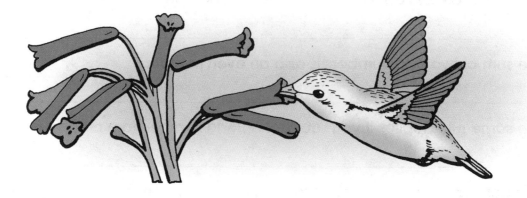

What do you know about the bee hummingbird, atlas moth, or capybara? Choose one, do some research, and write several sentences about it on a piece of paper. Then proofread your writing. Does every sentence begin and end correctly? Are all the words spelled correctly?

Spout Some Specifics

 To be a good writer, it is important to know what you are writing about, to be specific, and to include details. All this helps to create a picture for your readers and will make your writing more interesting and informative. Compare the two phrases below. Which one is more specific, interesting, and informative? Which one creates a more vivid picture?

a vehicle or *an old, rusty, dilapidated pick-up truck with flat tires and a shattered windshield*

For each general word or phrase, write a more specific word. Then add details to describe each specific word.

		Specific Word	Details
1.	a body of water	_____	_____
2.	a piece of furniture	_____	_____
3.	an article of clothing	_____	_____
4.	a child's toy	_____	_____
5.	a noise or sound	_____	_____
6.	a tool	_____	_____
7.	a group of people	_____	_____
8.	a reptile	_____	_____
9.	garden plants	_____	_____
10.	a kind of fruit	_____	_____
11.	a kind of vegetable	_____	_____
12.	a drink	_____	_____
13.	footwear	_____	_____
14.	musical instrument	_____	_____
15.	a holiday	_____	_____

 Look at yourself in the mirror. Then write on a piece of paper as many words and phrases as you can to describe yourself so that someone who does not know you would get a clear, vivid picture of what you look like.

Make It Interesting

A sentence can be very simple. This sentence tells who did what.

The crew worked.

As you write and revise your writing, add details about people, places, or things, or about where, when, and what happens. This will make your writing more interesting. Here's how the sentence above was revised several times. Each sentence gives a little more information.

The construction crew worked.
The construction crew worked quickly.
The construction crew worked quickly to clear the rubble.
The construction crew worked quickly to clear the rubble at the building site.
The construction crew worked quickly yesterday to clear the rubble at the building site.

Rewrite each sentence four times. Add new details each time to tell more about whom or what, how, where, and when.

The children played.

1. _____
   _____

2. _____
   _____

3. _____
   _____

4. _____
   _____

A package arrived.

1. _____
   _____

2. _____
   _____

3. _____
   _____

4. _____
   _____

Rewrite the following sentence several times on a piece of paper. Remove a detail each time until you are left with a very simple sentence.

The excited team cheered wildly after winning the championship basketball game.

Scholastic Teaching Resources

Order the Combination

*Have you ever noticed how short sentences can make your writing sound choppy? When two sentences have different subjects and the same predicate, you can use the conjunction **and** to combine them into one sentence with a compound subject.*

My friends ordered a pepperoni pizza. I ordered a pepperoni pizza.
My friends and I ordered a pepperoni pizza.

*When two sentences have the same subject and different predicates, you can use **and** to combine them into one sentence with a compound predicate.*

My mom ordered. She had pasta instead.
My mom ordered and had pasta instead.

*When two sentences have the same subject and predicate and different objects, you can combine them into one sentence with a compound object using **and**.*

My dad wanted anchovies on his pizza. He also wanted onions.
My dad wanted anchovies and onions on his pizza.

Fill in the missing subject, object, or predicate in each set of shorter sentences. Then combine the sentences by making compound subjects, objects, or predicates using *and*.

1. _____ are sweet and juicy.

   _____ are sweet and juicy.

   _____

2. I _____ about the history of basketball for homework.

   I _____ about the history of basketball for homework.

   _____

3. _____ is so much fun!

   _____ is also so much fun! (Change *is* to *are*.)

   _____

4. I like _____ more than broccoli or cauliflower.

   I like _____ more than broccoli or cauliflower.

   _____

5. I'd like to have _____ for breakfast.

   I'd also like to have _____ for breakfast.

   _____

A New Challenge

When you write, you may want to show how the ideas in two simple sentences are related. You can combine the two sentences by using a comma and the conjunctions **and**, **but**, *or* **or** *to show the connection.* **And** *shows a link between the ideas,* **but** *shows a contrast, and* **or** *shows a choice. The new sentence is called a* **compound sentence**.

> **My sister wants to join a football team. My parents aren't so happy about it.**
> **My sister wants to join a football team, <u>but</u> my parents aren't so happy about it.**
>
> **Annie is determined. Her friends think she'd make a great place kicker.**
> **Annie is determined, <u>and</u> her friends think she'd make a great place kicker.**
>
> **Should Annie play football? Should she try something else?**
> **Should Annie play football, <u>or</u> should she try something else?**

Combine each pair of sentences. Use *and, but,* or *or* to show the connection between the ideas and make a compound sentence.

1. My sister Annie has always participated in sports. Many say she's a natural athlete.

   _____

   _____

2. Soccer, basketball, and softball are fun. She wanted a new challenge.

   _____

   _____

3. My sister talked to my brother and me. We were honest with her.

   _____

   _____

4. I told Annie to go for it. My brother told her to stick with soccer or basketball.

   _____

   _____

5. Will Dad convince her to try skiing? Will he suggest ice skating?

   _____

   _____

Continue the story about Annie's choice on another piece of paper. Include some compound sentences to tell what happens. Make sure your sentences begin and end correctly. Remember to check for spelling errors.

Scholastic Teaching Resources

Hot Subjects

 If two sentences share the same subject, information about the subject can be written as a phrase after the subject in the new sentence. Be sure to use commas to set apart the phrase from the rest of the sentence.

Sentence 1: **The Gateway Arch is America's tallest human-made monument.**

Sentence 2: **The monument rises 630 feet above the ground.**

Combined: **The Gateway Arch, America's tallest human-made monument, rises 630 feet above the ground.**

Read the sentences. Combine the ideas in each pair into one sentence by including information in a phrase after the subject in the sentence.

1. The Caspian Sea is the world's largest lake.
The lake covers an area about the same size as Montana.

_____

2. The Komodo dragon is a member of the monitor family.
It can grow to a length of 10 feet.

_____

3. Our closest star is the sun.
It is estimated to be more than 27,000,000°F.

_____

4. Ronald W. Reagan was our nation's 40th president.
He worked as a Hollywood actor for almost 30 years.

_____

5. Georgia is the state that grows the most peanuts.
It harvests over 1.3 billion pounds each year.

_____

6. Hank Aaron is major league baseball's all-time home-run hitter.
He broke Babe Ruth's record in 1974.

_____

Sentence Building

 When you write about something, try to include interesting details. Sometimes you can take the important details from several related sentences and add them to the main sentence.

Kyle and Jim had a great plan.
They're my brothers.
The plan was for a tree house.

Now here's a sentence that combines all the important details.
My brothers Kyle and Jim had a great plan for a tree house.

Read each group of sentences. Take the important details from the two related sentences and add them to the main sentence to make one sentence.

1. My brothers built a tree house. They built it in the old oak tree. It's in our backyard.

   _____

2. Jim made a ladder for the tree house. He made it out of rope. It is sturdy.

   _____

3. Kyle bought paint. The paint was brown. He bought a gallon.

   _____

4. Kyle and Jim finished painting. They painted the walls. It took an hour.

   _____

5. Jim painted a sign. He painted "no trespassing." The sign is on the tree house door.

   _____

6. A squirrel leaped into their tree house. It leaped from a branch. It was curious.

   _____

7. The visitor startled my brothers. It was unexpected. My brothers were unsuspecting.

   _____

8. The squirrel leaped out of the tree house. It was frightened. It was in a big hurry.

   _____

 Write three short sentences on a piece of paper about a funny experience. Then try to combine them into one sentence. Which sounds better, one sentence with lots of details or two or three shorter sentences each with one detail? Why?

Applause for the Clause

 *Sometimes you can use words such as **when**, **because**, **while**, and **before** to combine two sentences with related ideas into one sentence with a main clause and a dependent clause. A* **clause** *is a group of words with a subject and a predicate. A* **dependent clause** *cannot stand alone. An* **independent clause** *can stand alone.*

Lee woke up late today. He realized he hadn't set the alarm last night.
When Lee woke up late today, he realized he hadn't set his alarm last night.

↑   ↑

This is a dependent clause.   *This is an independent clause.*

When the dependent clause comes before the main clause as in the above sentence, add a comma after the dependent clause. If the dependent clause follows the main clause, you do not need a comma. Here's an example.

Lee was upset. He was going to be late for school.
Lee was upset <u>because</u> he was going to be late for school.

Use the word inside the parentheses to combine each pair of sentences into one.

1. I waited for my parents to get home. I watched a movie. (while)

_____

2. My brother Alex was in his room. He had homework to do. (because)

_____

3. The movie was over. The power went out. (before)

_____

4. This happens all the time. I wasn't concerned. (since)

_____

5. I didn't mind the dark at first. I heard a scratching sound. (until)

_____

6. I found my flashlight. I started to look around. (when)

_____

7. I was checking the living room. I caught Alex trying to hide. (when)

_____

Triple the Fun

When you write, you may want to list three or more items or ideas in a series in a single sentence. Be sure to use a comma after each item in a series except after the last item.

Max dressed quickly, ate breakfast, and raced out the door.
Luis, Jamie, Leroy, and Sam met Max at the baseball field.
They were hopeful, excited, and nervous about their first game.

Answer each question below in a complete sentence. Use commas where they are needed. Make sure each sentence begins and ends correctly. Remember to check your spelling.

1. What are the titles of three books you've read recently or would like to read? Remember to underline the title of each book.

_____

2. What are four of the planets in our solar system closer to the sun than Pluto?

_____

3. What are three green, leafy vegetables?

_____

4. What countries would you like to visit? Include at least three in your answer.

_____

5. What months fall between January and July?

_____

6. What three things have you done today to help out at home?

_____

7. What states or bodies of water border your state?

_____

8. What activities do you and your friends enjoy in the summer?

_____

9. Who are some of the most important people in your life?

_____

Make up some questions like the ones above and challenge someone you know to answer them on a piece of paper. Correct the sentences.

Scholastic Teaching Resources

Comma Capers

 You know that you must use commas in a series of three or more items.
Max, Sam, and Alex ordered burgers, fries, and milkshakes for lunch.

Here are some additional rules you need to know about commas.
Use commas

— *to set off the name of the person or group you are addressing.*
Here's your order, boys.

— *after words like* yes, no, *and* well.
Well, what do you want to do now?

— *before a conjunction that joins two sentences.*
The boys finished lunch, and then they went to a movie.

Read the sentences below. Decide which ones need commas and which ones do not. Use this symbol ∧ to show where commas belong.

1. I'd like a bike a pair of in-line skates and a snowboard for my birthday.
2. Well my friend you can't always have what you want when you want it.
3. No but I can always hope!
4. My friends and I skate all year long and snowboard during the winter.
5. I used to like skateboarding but now I prefer snowboarding and in-line skating.
6. What sports games or hobbies do you enjoy most Jody?
7. I learned to ski last year and now I'm taking ice-skating lessons.
8. Skiing ice skating and skateboarding are all fun things to do.

Review the four rules above for using commas. Then write an original sentence for each rule. Begin and end each sentence correctly. Remember to check your spelling.

9. _____

10. _____

11. _____

12. _____

 Writers use commas for other reasons. As you read a newspaper, an article in your favorite magazine, a letter, or a book, look for examples of commas in sentences and jot them down on a piece of paper. Then see if you can figure out the rules.

Show Time

 Sometimes a writer can change the order of the words in a sentence to make it more interesting.

The telephone rang just as the girls were about to leave.
Just as the girls were about to leave, the phone rang.

Gina decided to answer it in spite of the time.
In spite of the time, Gina decided to answer it.

Do not forget to add a comma when you begin a sentence with a clause or a phrase that cannot stand alone as in the second and last sentences.

Rewrite each sentence by changing the order of the words.

1. Marta watched for the bus while Gina answered the phone.

2. The caller hung up just as Gina said, "Hello."

   _____

3. The girls were going to miss the one o'clock show unless they hurried.

   _____

4. The bus had already come and gone by the time they got to the corner.

   _____

5. The next bus to town finally showed up after the girls had waited a half hour.

   _____

6. The girls decided to catch the four o'clock show since they missed the earlier show.

   _____

7. They wouldn't have to stand in line later since Gina bought the tickets first.

   _____

8. Gina and Marta were at the theater by three o'clock even though it was early.

   _____

9. They bought a tub of popcorn and drinks once they were inside.

   _____

Keeps On Going

*Writers sometimes make the mistake of running together two or more sentences without telling how the ideas are related. This kind of sentence is called a **run-on sentence**.*

Kansas holds the record for having the largest ball of twine in the United States can you believe it weighs over 17,000 pounds in fact, the giant ball is 40 feet in circumference, 11 feet tall, and made up of more than 1,100 miles of twine!

To fix a run-on sentence, identify each complete thought or idea and break it into shorter sentences.

Kansas holds the record for having the largest ball of twine in the United States. Can you believe it weighs over 17,000 pounds? In fact, the giant ball is 40 feet in circumference, 11 feet tall, and made up of more than 1,100 miles of twine!

Rewrite each run-on sentence correctly. Remember to begin and end each sentence correctly.

1. Did you know that the United States is the top meat-eating country in the world each person consumes about 260 pounds of meat each year beef is the most commonly eaten meat.

    _____

    _____

    _____

2. Have you ever noticed that Abraham Lincoln faces right on a penny he is the only president on a U.S. coin who does Sacagawea faces right on the new dollar coin, but she was not a president?

    _____

    _____

    _____

3. It would be fantastic to have a robot to do all my chores, help do my homework, and play games I really think the day will come unfortunately, it won't come soon enough for me.

    _____

    _____

    _____

A Long School Year

 Have you ever accidentally left out words when you write? Whenever you write, it is always a good idea to proofread for words that may be missing. Here is an example of what to do when you want to add a missing word as you proofread.

     e-mail
I got an ˄ from my friend last night.

    met
We ˄ last summer when my family was in Japan.

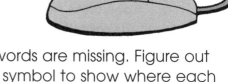

Read the passage below about school in Japan. Twenty words are missing. Figure out what they are and add them to the sentences. Use the ˄ symbol to show where each missing word belongs. Then write each missing word above the sentence.
Hint: Every sentence has at least one missing word.

      How would like to go to school on Saturdays? If you lived in the of Japan,

that's just where you'd be each Saturday morning. I have a who lives in Japan.

Yuichi explained that attend classes five and one-half a week. The day is on

Saturday. I was also surprised to that the Japanese school is one of the longest

in the world—over 240 days. It begins in the of April. While we have over two

months off each, students in Japan get their in late July and August. School

then again in fall and ends in March. The people of believe that a good is very

important. Children are required to attend school from the age of six to the of

fifteen. They have elementary and middle just like we do. Then most students go

on to school for another three years. Yuichi says that students work very because

the standards are so high. He and some of his friends even extra classes after

school. They all want to get into a good someday.

 Write several sentences about something that interests you on a piece of paper. Rewrite the sentences on another piece of paper, this time leaving out a key word in each one. Challenge someone you know to add the missing words. Then compare the two sets of sentences.

Scholastic Teaching Resources

Parts of a Paragraph

A **paragraph** *is a group of sentences that tells about one main idea. The* **topic sentence** *tells the main idea and is usually the first sentence.* **Supporting sentences** *tell more about the main idea. The* **closing sentence** *of a paragraph often retells the main idea in a different way. Here are the parts for one paragraph.*

Paragraph Title: **Starting Over**

Topic Sentence: **Today started off badly and only got worse.**

Supporting Sentences: 1. **Everyone in my family woke up late this morning.**

2. **I had only 15 minutes to get ready and catch the bus.**

3. **I dressed as fast as I could, grabbed an apple and my backpack, and raced to get to the bus stop on time.**

4. **Fortunately, I just made it.**

5. **Unfortunately, the bus was pulling away when several kids pointed out that I had on two different shoes.**

Closing Sentence: **At that moment, I wanted to start the day over.**

When you write a paragraph, remember these rules:

• **Indent** *the first line to let readers know that you are beginning a paragraph.*

• **Capitalize** *the first word of each sentence.*

• **Punctuate** *each sentence correctly (? ! . ,).*

Use all the information above to write the paragraph. Be sure to follow the rules.

_____

paragraph title

_____

_____

_____

_____

_____

_____

_____

_____

What's the Topic?

 Every paragraph has a topic sentence that tells the main idea of the paragraph, or what it is about. It usually answers several of these questions:

Who?   What?   Where?   When?   Why?   How?

Here are some examples.

The doe and her fawn faced many dangers in the forest.
We were amazed by our guest's rude behavior.
Baking bread from scratch is really not so difficult, or so I thought.
Getting up in the morning is the hardest thing to do.

Did these topic sentences grab your attention? A good topic sentence should.

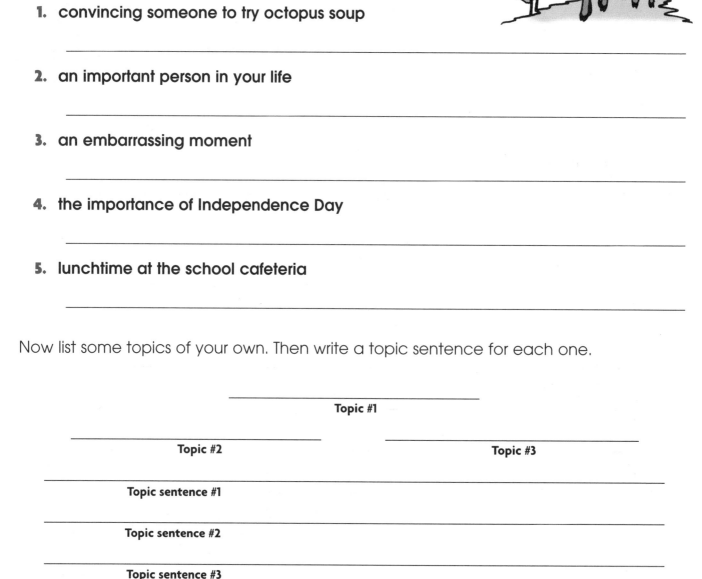

Here are some topics. Write a topic sentence for each one.

1. convincing someone to try octopus soup

_____

2. an important person in your life

_____

3. an embarrassing moment

_____

4. the importance of Independence Day

_____

5. lunchtime at the school cafeteria

_____

Now list some topics of your own. Then write a topic sentence for each one.

_____
Topic #1

_____   _____
Topic #2   **Topic #3**

_____
Topic sentence #1

_____
Topic sentence #2

_____
Topic sentence #3

Topic Talk

Most paragraphs begin with a topic sentence, but it can appear elsewhere in a paragraph. Sometimes a topic sentence is located at the end of a paragraph or even in the middle.

A boiling mass of clouds was almost overhead. A bolt of lightning streaked across the darkened sky. Thunder boomed, and it began to rain and hail. <u>We had to find a safe place quickly!</u> There wasn't a moment to spare because early summer storms sometimes turn into tornadoes.

Read the paragraph again. This time try the topic sentence elsewhere in the paragraph.

Read each paragraph. Notice that each one is missing a topic sentence. Think about the supporting sentences. What main idea do you think they support? Write a topic sentence to tell the main idea of each paragraph. Remember that a topic sentence is not always the first sentence of a paragraph.

1. The days are growing longer. The winter snows are melting as the temperatures rise. Colorful crocuses are popping up here and there. Robins have begun to return north, and creatures are beginning to come out of their winter burrows. _____

    _____

2. _____

    It was fun and easy. Students, parents, and teachers began saving the box tops from all Healthful Foods products. After we collected 100,000 box tops, we mailed them to Healthful Foods headquarters. We earned 10 cents for each box top for a total of $10,000. Our school will use the money to buy computers.

3. The last weekend in June is quickly approaching. You know what that means.

    _____

    This year the festivities will begin at 10:00 A.M. at Twin Lakes Picnic Grove, pavilion 12. As always, there will be music, dancing, lots of great food, games, and some new surprises! We look forward to seeing you.

A Lot of Details

 When you are ready to write a topic sentence, think about the main topic or idea of the paragraph you will be writing and the details you plan to include. Then jot down several possible sentences and choose the best one. Remember that a topic sentence can answer several questions: Who? What? Where? When? Why? How?

Tony Hawk
- skateboarder
- in his thirties
- turned professional at age 14
- has won more skateboarding contests than anyone
- made history at Summer X Games in 1999—landed a "900"
  (a complete somersault done 2 $\frac{1}{2}$ times in midair)

Possible topic sentences: **There is no other skateboarder like Tony Hawk.**
Tony Hawk is an extraordinary skateboarder.
Tony Hawk is the "old man" of skateboarding.

Here are some topics with details. Write two topic sentences for each one on the lines below.

1. **Pet Rocks**	2. **Komodo Dragon**	3. **A Great Dessert**
— fad in the 1970s — idea came from Gary Dahl, a salesman — sold rocks as pets — came with a manual — manual had tips on how to teach a pet rock tricks	— member of monitor family — grows to 10 feet and weighs 300 pounds — meat eater — dangerous to humans — largest lizard in the world — long neck and tail, strong legs — found on Komodo Island	— slice a banana — add vanilla ice cream — sprinkle on some walnuts — cover with lots of hot fudge sauce — top with mounds of whipped cream and a cherry

1. _____

_____

2. _____

_____

3. _____

_____

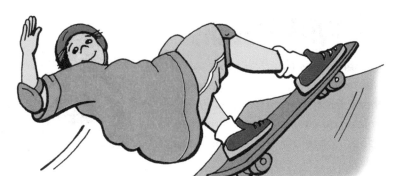

Remember that the supporting sentences you write support or tell more about the main idea in your topic sentence. Read the paragraph below. Draw one line under the <u>topic sentence</u>. Draw two lines under the <u>supporting sentences</u>. Check (√) the closing sentence.

Tony Hawk

Tony Hawk is an extraordinary skateboarder. He turned professional when he was only 14 years old. Now in his thirties, Tony has won more skateboarding contests than anyone else has. He even made history in 1999 by landing a trick called the "900" at the Summer X Games. Tony Hawk may just be the greatest skateboarder in the world.

Now, review the topics on page 26. Choose one. Then review the details listed about the topic in the box. Next, use the information to write at least three supporting sentences to support the topic sentence you wrote. Include a closing sentence and a title. Write the paragraph below.

_____

_____

_____

_____

_____

_____

Make a list of topics you would like to write about. Choose one. Then list on a piece of paper details you know about the topic. Do some research if necessary. Then write a topic sentence and several supporting sentences.

Drizzle With Details

A good paragraph needs supporting sentences that tell more about the main idea of the topic sentence. Supporting sentences are sometimes called detail sentences. Every detail sentence in a paragraph must relate to the main idea. In the following paragraph, the one supporting sentence that does not relate to the main idea has been underlined.

My first day of softball practice was a total disaster! Not only was I ten minutes late, but I also forgot my glove. Then during batting practice, I missed the ball every time I took a swing. I definitely have improved on my catching skills. To make matters even worse, I tripped in the outfield and twisted my ankle. I was definitely not off to a very good start.

Read the following paragraph. Underline the topic sentence. Then cross out any supporting sentences that do not relate to the main idea.

Yesterday our science class went on a field trip to a pond. Next month we're going to the ocean. That will be fun. We've been studying the pond as an ecosystem in class. Our teacher wanted us to observe firsthand all the different habitats in and around the pond. She had us keep a checklist of the different kinds of plants and animals in each pond habitat. One of the boys accidentally fell in. He was really embarrassed. Along the water's edge I saw several kinds of plants partly underwater, two salamanders, snails, and water bugs. I observed many different habitats.

Read the title and topic sentence for each of the following paragraph plans. Then write four supporting sentences that relate to and support each one.

1. **Paragraph Title:**   Uniforms—To Wear or Not to Wear?
   Topic Sentence: Our school should require all students to wear uniforms.

   Supporting Sentences:

   1. _____
   2. _____
   3. _____
   4. _____

2. **Paragraph Title:**   An Adventure in Dreamland
   Topic Sentence: Last night I had the most incredible dream.

   Supporting Sentences:

   1. _____
   2. _____
   3. _____
   4. _____

3. **Paragraph Title:**   A Sad Day
   Topic Sentence: I will always remember how sad I was that day.

   Supporting Sentences:

   1. _____
   2. _____
   3. _____
   4. _____

 Choose one of the titles and topic sentences above. On a piece of paper, write a paragraph using the supporting sentences you wrote above. Include more supporting sentences that relate to the topic sentence if you want. Then add a closing sentence. Remember to indent, begin and end sentences correctly, punctuate correctly, and check your spelling.

A Musical Lesson

*There are many kinds of paragraphs. When you write a **comparison paragraph**, you compare by telling how things are similar and contrast by telling how things are different. You can use a Venn diagram to help organize your ideas. Here is an example.*

Trumpet	Both	Violin
• brass • has a mouthpiece • has three valves	• are played in orchestras • musical instruments • take practice	• wood • four strings • played with a bow

Complete the paragraph using details to compare and contrast the trumpet and violin. Remember to capitalize and punctuate correctly.

Trumpet Versus Violin

The trumpet and violin are both musical instruments that are _____

_____. However, there are some

important differences. The trumpet _____

_____

_____

_____

On the other hand, the violin _____

_____

_____

_____

Both instruments _____

_____

Make a list on a piece of paper of things to compare and contrast such as a house and an apartment building, ice skating and skateboarding, or spinach and broccoli. Choose one pair. Make and complete a Venn diagram like the one above. Then write a paragraph to tell how they are similar and different.

Is That a Fact?

*What is the difference between a fact and an opinion? A **fact** can be checked or proven. An opinion is what someone believes or feels about something. An **opinion** cannot be proven.*

Fact → **Cocoa beans are used to make chocolate.**

Opinion → **Chocolate pudding is better than chocolate ice cream.**

Read each sentence. Write *F* next to each fact. Write *O* next to each opinion.

_____ **1.** Everyone in the world thinks chocolate makes the best candy.

_____ **2.** In Switzerland, the average person eats about 22 pounds of chocolate in a year.

_____ **3.** That means the Swiss eat about 160 million pounds of chocolate annually.

_____ **4.** I think Americans eat more chocolate than that.

_____ **5.** People also use chocolate to make drinks and to flavor recipes.

_____ **6.** There's nothing better than a chocolate donut with chocolate glaze.

Look at the pictures. Then write two facts and two opinions about each snack food. Use clue words such as *think, best, believe, like,* and *dislike* to signal an opinion.

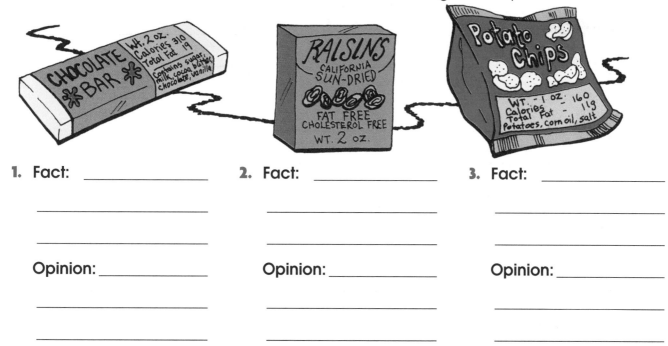

1. Fact: _____

_____

_____

Opinion: _____

_____

_____

2. Fact: _____

_____

_____

Opinion: _____

_____

_____

3. Fact: _____

_____

_____

Opinion: _____

_____

_____

As you listen to a conversation among your friends about an issue that is important to them, try to identify the facts and opinions you hear and write them down on a piece of paper. Then ask, "Can this statement be proven?" If the answer is yes, then it is a fact. If not, then it is an opinion. Circle any clue words or phrases that signal opinions.

I'm Convinced!

*In a **persuasive paragraph**, you give an opinion about something and try to convince readers to think or feel the way you do. A convincing persuasive paragraph includes*

— **a topic sentence that clearly states your opinion.**
— **reasons that support your opinion.**
— **facts to back up your opinion.**
— **a strong closing sentence that summarizes your opinion.**

Pretend you are a world-famous chef who prepares dishes that include edible insects—insects that you can eat. You want to persuade people to include insects in their diet. Here is a topic sentence for a persuasive paragraph.

Everyone should try cooking with insects.

Here are some reasons and facts.
• Many insects like mealworms, crickets, and weevils are edible.
• People in many cultures around the world eat insects.
• Many insects are low in fat and rich in vitamins.
• Lots of tasty recipes include insects.
• Insects are really quite delicious.

Now put it all together. Write a persuasive paragraph that includes a title and a strong closing sentence. Remember the rules for writing a paragraph.

Paragraph Title: _____

Topic Sentence: _____

_____

Reasons/Facts: _____

_____

_____

_____

_____

_____

_____

_____

Closing Sentence: _____

_____

Step by Step

 When you write an **expository paragraph***, you give facts and information, explain ideas, or give directions. An expository paragraph can also include opinions. Here are some topic ideas for an expository paragraph.*

Explain how to play the flute.   **Explain how to bathe a dog.**
Tell why you do not like brussels sprouts.   **Tell what skills you need to skateboard.**
Give facts about yourself.   **Give the facts about your favorite band.**

Here is an example of an expository paragraph. It explains how to fry an egg.

Frying an egg is not all that difficult. After melting a little bit of butter in a frying pan, just crack the eggshell along the rim of the pan and let the egg drop into the pan. Do it gently so the yolk does not break. Let the egg fry over a low heat for about a minute or so. That is all it takes.

Complete the following topics for expository paragraphs with your own ideas.

Explain how to	Give facts about	Tell why
_____	_____	_____
_____	_____	_____
_____	_____	_____

Use the form below to develop one of your ideas for an expository paragraph.

Paragraph Title: _____

Topic Sentence: _____

_____

Details/Facts/Steps: _____

_____

_____

_____

_____

Closing Sentence: _____

_____

Now, use the plan above to write a paragraph on a piece of paper. If you are giving directions for doing or making something, include words such as *first, next, after that,* and *finally* to make the steps clear for your readers.

A Sentence Relationship

*You can write sentences about cause and effect relationships. A **cause** is the reason why something happens. An **effect** is the result of the cause, or what actually happens. Words such as **so**, **because**, and **since** are used in cause and effect sentences.*

      effect   *cause*

School was cancelled today <u>because</u> the storm dumped two feet of snow.

        cause   *effect*

The snow and wind knocked out power lines, <u>so</u> many homes were without electricity.

        cause   *effect*

<u>Since</u> there was no school today, I went back to bed and slept another hour.

Add a cause to each of the following sentences about the day that school was cancelled because of snow.

1. Many shops, stores, and offices were closed _____

_____

2. My friends and I love snow days _____

_____

3. It took several minutes to open the back door _____

_____

4. Our snow blower would not start _____

_____

Add an effect to each of the following sentences.

5. I shoveled snow for two hours, _____

_____

6. My sister could not find her boots, _____

_____

7. Since our street was finally plowed by noon, _____

_____

8. By late afternoon it began snowing again, _____

_____

What a Mess!

 *You can write a paragraph using a cause and effect
relationship. One way to begin is to state a cause. Then you
write about the effects that happen as a result of that cause.*

**The piercing sound of the smoke alarm
reminded Max that he had forgotten to check
the pot of stew heating up on the stove. The
stew had boiled over, the bottom of the pot was
scorched, and smoke was filling the kitchen.
Dinner was obviously ruined, and Max was in big
trouble. What a mess!**

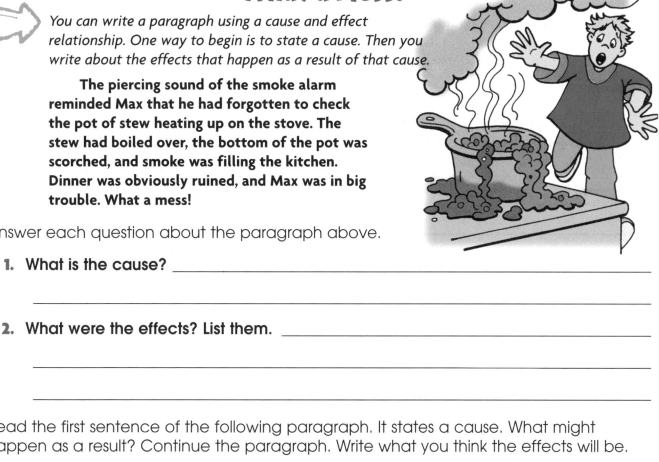

Answer each question about the paragraph above.

1. **What is the cause?** _____

_____

2. **What were the effects? List them.** _____

_____

_____

Read the first sentence of the following paragraph. It states a cause. What might
happen as a result? Continue the paragraph. Write what you think the effects will be.

I walked into my room just as Sebastian, our very inquisitive cat, managed

to tip over the goldfish bowl that had been on my desk. _____

_____

_____

_____

_____

_____

 Brainstorm a list of causes on a piece of paper. Here are some to get you started:
eating too many cookies   staying up too late   not studying for a test
Then list some possible effects. Develop your ideas into a paragraph.

A Vivid Picture

 A **descriptive paragraph** *creates a vivid image or picture for readers. By choosing just the right adjectives, you can reveal how something looks, sounds, smells, tastes, and feels. Compare the sentences from two different paragraphs. Which one creates a more vivid picture?*

The pizza with sausage and onions tasted so good.

The smooth, sweet sauce and bubbly mozzarella topped with bite-sized chunks of extra-hot sausage and thin slivers of sweet onion on a perfectly baked, thin crust delighted my taste buds.

Cut out a picture of something interesting and paste it in the box. Then brainstorm a list adjectives and descriptive phrases to tell about it.

_____ _____

_____ _____

_____ _____

_____ _____

_____ _____

Now, write a paragraph about the picture. Begin your paragraph with a topic sentence that will grab readers. Add supporting sentences that include the adjectives and descriptive phrases listed to create a vivid picture.

_____

_____

_____

_____

_____

 Here is a set of adjectives: *bumpy, dusty, narrow, steep, curvy, unpaved, well-worn*. **Think about what they might describe. Then, on a piece of paper use the words to write a descriptive paragraph that paints a picture.**

Scholastic Teaching Resources

Numerous, Spectacular Words

When you write, do you sometimes overuse descriptive words like **good**, **bad**, **nice**, *or* **wonderful**? *Overused words can make your writing boring.*

> *The weather was* **good** *for our first camping trip. (fair)*
> *A ranger gave us some really* **good** *tips about the park. (useful)*
> *Mom thought the campsite near the stream was* **good**. *(lovely)*
> *My older brother is a* **good** *fly fisherman. (skilled)*
> *He said his equipment is too* **good** *for me to use, though! (valuable)*

Now reread the sentences. This time use the words in parentheses in place of the word **good**. *You can use a thesaurus to help find words. A thesaurus is a reference book that gives synonyms and antonyms for words.*

Identify eight frequently overused descriptive words in the passage below and list them in the answer spaces. Next, use a thesaurus to write three synonyms for each word, or write three synonyms you know. Then revise the passage. Use editing symbols to cross out the overused words and add the more effective synonyms to replace them.

> **Our family has a dog named Scooter. He's normally very good until it's time to bathe him. That's when our nice, little terrier turns into a big, furry monster. Scooter isn't really bad. He's just hard to handle when he doesn't want to do something. I think he's afraid of water. You should see how sad he looks once we manage to get him into the tub.**

1. _____ _____
2. _____ _____
3. _____ _____
4. _____ _____
5. _____ _____
6. _____ _____
7. _____ _____
8. _____ _____

Reread a composition you have recently written. Look for overused words and then use a thesaurus to find other words that you could use instead to make your writing more interesting.

Action Alert

 When you write, think about the verbs that you choose to express action in your sentences. Are they as exact as they can be? Do they tell your readers exactly what you want to say?

The child **broke** the plastic toy.
The child **smashed** the plastic toy.
The child **cracked** the plastic toy.

Each verb creates a different picture of what happened.

Read each sentence. Underline the verb. Then rewrite each sentence using a more exact verb. You may want to use a thesaurus.

1. Three young hikers went up the steep hill.

_____

2. A lone runner ran around the track.

_____

3. The wind blew through the treetops.

_____

4. The janitor cleaned the scuff marks off the floor.

_____

5. The audience laughed at the hilarious scene.

_____

6. The diners ate the delicious meal.

_____

7. The young tourists liked the castle most of all.

_____

8. The children slept for about an hour.

_____

9. The biologist looked at the unusual specimen.

_____

 Here are some commonly used verbs: *make, tell, say, speak, ride.* **On a piece of paper, list as many exact verbs as you can think of for each one. Use a thesaurus for additional words. Then write several sentences using the exact words on your list.**

Scholastic Teaching Resources

Colorful Clues

*You can compare two things that are not alike in order to give your readers a clearer and more colorful picture. When you use **like** or **as** to make a comparison, it is called a **simile**.*

Max is as slow as molasses when he doesn't want to do something.
My sister leaped over the puddles like a frog to avoid getting her shoes wet.
The angry man erupted like a volcano.

*When you make a comparison without **like** or **as**, it is called a **metaphor**. You compare things directly, saying the subject is something else.*

The disturbed anthill was a whirlwind of activity.
The oak trees, silent sentries around the cabin, stood guard.
Jenny and I were all ears as we listened to the latest gossip.

Finish the metaphors and similes.

1. Crowds of commuters piled into the subway cars like _____

   _____

2. Chirping crickets on warm summer night are _____

   _____

3. After rolling in the mud, our dog looked like _____

4. Happiness is _____

5. Just learning to walk, the toddler was as wobbly as _____

   _____

6. After scoring the winning point, I felt as _____

   _____

7. Having a tooth filled is about as much fun as _____

   _____

8. A summer thunderstorm is _____

   _____

9. _____ is _____

10. _____ is like _____

Scholastic Teaching Resources

Adding Spice

 Sometimes you can spice up your writing by giving human characteristics and qualities to non-human things such as animals and objects. This is called **personification**.

> **The sagging roof groaned under the weight of all the snow.**
> **The falling leaves danced in the wind.**

You can also use **hyperbole**, *or deliberate exaggeration, to make a point clearer or to add drama to your writing.*

> **The lost hiker is so hungry he could eat a bear.**
> **Yesterday was so hot, we could have fried eggs on the sidewalk.**

Personify the animal or object in each sentence by giving it human qualities.

1. **The rusted hinges on the old wooden door** _____

   _____

2. **As several birds began feasting on the farmer's corn, the scarecrow** _____

   _____

3. **A gentle summer breeze** _____

   _____

4. **Just as I walked past the statue of Ben Franklin, it** _____

   _____

Complete each sentence with an example of a hyperbole.

5. **The salsa was so spicy hot** _____

   _____

6. **The pumpkin grew so large** _____

   _____

7. **If we placed all the books in the library end to end, they** _____

   _____

8. **My room was so cold last night that by morning** _____

   _____

 Listen for examples of hyperbole in the conversations that you hear throughout the day. Jot them down in a notebook. Then make up some of your own.

Scholastic Teaching Resources

Daily Notes

When you keep a journal, you can record the facts and details about events that happen in your life and your feelings or opinions about them. Your journal entries can be a valuable resource when you are looking for writing ideas.

3/9 We had to take Fuzzer to his new home today. Our new landlord said he could not stay with us at our apartment anymore. I know Fuzzer will be much happier at the farm where he can run and play, but I still felt so sad. I tried not to cry, but I could not help it. Fuzzer has been part of our family for nine years. We grew up together. I will miss him very much!

3/15 I had to go to my sister's dance recital at the Palace Theater last night. She performed in three numbers. At first I didn't want to go because I thought it would be boring, but it wasn't. I actually felt really proud of my sister! She was fantastic. I guess I really should tell her.

3/19 Today, the entire fourth grade went on a field trip to the state capital. It was incredible! We met a state senator. She showed us around the capitol building. We even got to listen to the senators discuss a new law. Later, we toured the governor's mansion. Boy, is that a big house!

Think about the events that have happened in your life over the last several days. Did anything of special importance happen at home, on the way to or from school, or in your community, the country, or the world? Record the facts, details, and your feelings or opinions about two events on the journal page below. Write the date for each entry.

_____/_____/_____

_____

_____

_____

_____

_____/_____/_____

_____

_____

_____

_____

Story Time

*A story has **characters**, a **setting** (where and when the story takes place), and a **plot** (the events that happen in a story). The main story character often faces a problem which is introduced at the **beginning** of a story, developed in the **middle**, and solved at the **end**.*

Develop your own story about the picture. First, answer the questions.

1. **What or who is the story about?** _____

_____

_____

_____

2. **Where and when does it take place?** _____

_____

_____

_____

3. **How will the story begin?** _____

_____

_____

_____

4. **What happens in the middle?** _____

_____

_____

5. **How will the story end?** _____

_____

_____

Use your answers to write a story on another sheet of paper. Include a title. Be sure to tell the events in the order they happen. Remember the rules for writing a paragraph.

Compile magazine pictures that spark story ideas. From time to time choose one of the pictures and make up an oral story about it. If you have an audiocassette recorder, tape your story and save it. Use it to write a story at another time.

Scholastic Teaching Resources

What Did You Say?

Some stories may include dialogue, or the exact words of story characters. Dialogue lets readers know something about the characters, plot, setting, and problem or conflict in a story. Use quotation marks around a speaker's exact words and commas to set off quotations. Remember to put periods, question marks, exclamation points, and commas inside the quotation marks.

"Get away from my bowl!" yelled Little Miss Muffet when she saw the approaching spider.

"Please don't get so excited," replied the startled spider. "I just wanted a little taste. I've never tried curds and whey before."

Use your imagination to complete the dialogue between the fairy tale or nursery rhyme characters. Include quotation marks and commas where they belong and the correct end punctuation.

1. When Baby Bear saw the strange girl asleep in his bed, he asked his parents, _____

   _____

   His mother replied, _____

2. Humpty Dumpty was sitting on the wall when he suddenly fell off. On the way down

   he shouted, _____

   Two of the king's men approached. One whispered nervously to the other, _____

   _____

3. When Jack realized he was about to fall down the hill with a pail of water, he

   yelled, _____

   _____ cried Jill,

   as she went tumbling down the hill after Jack.

4. The wolf knocked on the door of the third little pig's house. When there was no

   answer, the wolf bellowed, _____

   Knowing that he and his brother were safe inside his sturdy brick house, the third

   little pig replied, _____

   _____

Let's Get Organized

When you write a report or story, it helps to review your notes and organize them into an outline to show the order in which you want to discuss them.

Chester Greenwood → *subject of the report*

I. **Who was Chester Greenwood?** → *main idea becomes topic sentence*
   A. **born in 1858** → *supporting details become supporting sentences*
   B. **grew up in Farmington, Maine**
   C. **as a child had ear problems in winter**

II. **His first invention—earmuffs**
   A. **needed a way to protect ears from cold**
   B. **1873 at age 15 began testing his ideas**
   C. **idea for fur-covered earflaps worked**
   D. **people saw and also wanted earflaps**
   E. **grandmother helped produce them**

III. **His later accomplishments**
   A. **founded a telephone company**
   B. **manufactured steam heaters**
   C. **over 100 inventions**

Study the outline above. Then answer the questions.

1. What is the topic of the report? _____

2. How many paragraphs will there be? _____

3. What is the main topic of the first paragraph? _____

_____

4. How many details tell about the second main idea? _____

Use the form on the next page to develop an outline for preparing an interesting and unusual dish that your family enjoys.

How to Prepare _____

  I. **Background about the dish**

      A. _____

      B. _____

      C. _____

      D. _____

      E. _____

  II. **Ingredients**

      A. _____

      B. _____

      C. _____

      D. _____

      E. _____

  III. **Equipment**

      A. _____

      B. _____

      C. _____

      D. _____

      E. _____

  IV. **Steps**

      A. _____

      B. _____

      C. _____

      D. _____

      E. _____

Share your outline with someone you know.

Read All About It

 A **news story** *reports just the facts about an event and answers the questions* **who**, **what**, **when**, **where**, **why**, *and* **how**. *The most important information is included at the beginning of the article in a paragraph called the* **lead**.

Grass Fires Burn Out of Control ← headline

WHERE did it happen? →

GREENSBURG—Grass fires, fueled by wind gusts up to 50 miles per hour, spread into a residential area early Tuesday morning. All residents had to be evacuated. Within minutes over 25 homes were engulfed by flames and destroyed. According to officials, no injuries have been reported.

Planes and helicopters battling the blaze had to be grounded because the heat of the flames was so intense.

WHY did it happen?

WHEN did it happen?

WHO was affected?

Write a news story using the information below. Remember to write about the facts and events in the order they occurred. Follow the model lead above.

Who: Roseville Emergency Rescue Team
When: April 10, 2003; 5 A.M.
Where: Slate Run River
What: team and rescue vehicles sent;
    worked for three hours; rescued residents
How: used helicopter and boats
Why: residents along river stranded by flash flood after storm

_____

_____ — _____

_____

_____

_____

_____

_____

 Use your imagination to write a news story on a piece of paper for one of the following headlines or one of your own.

Mystery of the Missing Dinosaur Solved   **Students Protest School Lunch Menu**

City High Wins Championship   **First Female Elected President**

Answer Key

Page 5
Sentences will vary.

Page 6
A. (left to right) S, P; S, P; P, P; S, P; S, S; P, S; P, P; S, S; B. 1. Half a loaf is better than none. 2. One good turn deserves another. 3. One rotten apple spoils the whole barrel. 4. The show must go on. 5. Every cloud has a silver lining. 6. The early bird catches the worm. 7. A rolling stone gathers no moss. 8. Haste makes waste.

Page 7
1. S; 2. E; 3. S; 4. Q; 5. C; 6. E; 7. C; 8. E; 9. Q; 10. C; 11. S; 12. Q

Page 8
1. Did you know that the whale shark can grow to a length of 60 feet? 2. That's about as long as two school buses parked end to end! 3. These huge creatures are not a threat to humans like some other sharks are. 4. Whale sharks float near the surface to look for plankton and tiny fish. 5. Imagine how amazing it must be to swim alongside a whale shark. 6. There are an estimated 20,000 known species of fish in the world. 7. Is the dwarf pygmy goby the smallest of all these species? 8. This species of goby is less than a half-inch long when it is fully grown! 9. This tiny fish makes its home in the massive Indian Ocean.

Page 9
1. Are numbers that cannot be divided evenly by 2 called odd numbers? 2. Can all even numbers be divided evenly by 2? 3. Is 0 considered an even number? 4. Are numbers that have 0, 2, 4, 6, or 8 in the ones place even numbers? 5. Do odd numbers end in 1, 3, 5, 7, or 9? 6. Is the number 317,592 an even number because it ends in 2? 7. Is the sum always an even number when you add two even numbers? 8. Is the sum of two odd numbers also an even number? 9. Does the same rule apply if you subtract an odd number from an odd number? 10. Can you figure out all the rules for working with odd and even numbers?

Page 10
Think about the fastest car you've ever seen in the Indianapolis 500 race. That's about how fast a peregrine falcon dives. It actually reaches speeds up to 175 miles an hour. How incredibly fast they are! Peregrine falcons are also very powerful birds. Did you know that they can catch and kill their prey in the air using their sharp claws? What's really amazing is that peregrine falcons live in both the country and in the city. Keep on the lookout if you're ever in New York City. Believe it or not, it is home to a very large population of falcons.

Page 11
Answers will vary.

Page 12
Sentences will vary. Bonus: The simple sentence will be: The team cheered.

Page 13
Answers and sentences will vary.

Page 14
1. My sister Annie has always participated in sports, and many say she's a natural athlete. 2. Soccer, basketball, and softball are fun, but she wanted a new challenge. 3. My sister talked to my brother and me, and we were honest with her. 4. I told Annie to go for it, but my brother told her to stick with soccer or basketball. 5. Will Dad convince her to try skiing, or will he suggest ice skating?

Page 15
1. The Caspian Sea, the world's largest lake, covers an area about the same size as Montana. 2. The Komodo dragon, a member of the monitor family, can grow to a length of 10 feet. 3. Our closest star, the sun, is estimated to be more than 27,000,000°F. 4. Ronald W. Reagan, our nation's 40th president, worked as a Hollywood actor for almost 30 years. 5. Georgia, the state that grows the most peanuts, harvests over 1.3 billion pounds each year. 6. Hank Aaron, major league baseball's all-time home-run hitter, broke Babe Ruth's record in 1974.

Page 16
1. My brothers built a tree house in the old oak tree in our backyard. 2. Jim made a sturdy rope ladder for the tree house. 3. Kyle bought a gallon of brown paint. 4. Kyle and Jim finished painting the walls in an hour. 5. Jim painted a "no trespassing" sign on the tree house door. 6. A curious squirrel leaped from a branch into their tree house. 7. The unexpected visitor startled my unsuspecting brothers. 8. The frightened squirrel leaped out of the tree house in a big hurry.

Page 17
1. While I waited for my parents to get home, I watched a movie. 2. My brother Alex was in his room because he had homework to do. 3. Before the movie was over, the power went out. 4. Since this happens all the time, I wasn't concerned. 5. I didn't mind the dark at first until I heard a scratching sound. 6. When I found my flashlight, I started to look around. 7. I was checking the living room when I caught Alex trying to hide.

Page 18
Sentences will vary.

Page 19
1. I'd like a bike, a pair of in-line skates, and a snowboard for my birthday. 2. Well, my friend, you can't always have what you want when you want it. 3. No, but I can always hope! 4. My friends and I skate all year long and snowboard during the winter. 5. I used to like skateboarding, but now I prefer snowboarding and in-line skating. 6. What sports, games, or hobbies do you enjoy most, Jody? 7. I learned to ski last year, and now I'm taking ice-skating lessons. 8. Skiing, ice skating, and skateboarding are all fun things to do. 9–12: Sentences will vary.

Page 20
1. While Gina answered the phone, Marta watched for the bus. 2. Just as Gina said, "Hello," the caller hung up. 3. Unless they hurried, the girls were going to miss the one o'clock show. 4. By the time they got to the corner, the bus had already come and gone. 5. After the girls had waited a half hour, the next bus to town finally showed up. 6. Since they missed the earlier show, the girls decided to catch the four o'clock show. 7. Since Gina bought the tickets first, they wouldn't have to stand in line later. 8. Even though it was early, Gina and Marta were at the theater by three o'clock. 9. Once they were inside, they bought a tub of popcorn and drinks.

Page 21
Possible sentences: 1. Did you know that the United States is the top meat-eating country in the world? Each person consumes about 260 pounds of meat each year. Beef is the most commonly eaten meat. 2. Have you ever noticed that Abraham Lincoln faces right on a penny? He is the only president on a U.S. coin who does. Sacagawea faces right on the new dollar coin, but she was not a president. 3. It would be fantastic to have a robot to do all my chores, help do my homework, and play games. I really think the day will come. Unfortunately, it won't come soon enough for me.

Page 22

How would **you** like to go to school on Saturdays? If you lived in the **country** of Japan, that's just where you'd be each Saturday morning. I have a **friend** who lives in Japan. Yuichi explained that **students** attend classes five and one-half **days** a week. The **half** day is on Saturday. I was also surprised to **learn** that the Japanese school **year** is one of the longest in the world—over 240 days. It begins in the **month** of April. While we have over two months off each **summer**, students in Japan get their **vacation** in late July and August. School then **begins** again in fall and ends in March. The people of **Japan** believe that a good **education** is very important. Children are required to attend school from the age of six to the **age** of fifteen. They have elementary and middle **schools** just like we do. Then most students go on to **high** school for another three years. Yuichi says that students work very **hard** because the standards are so high. He and some of his friends even **take** extra classes after school. They all want to get into a good **college** someday.

Page 23

Starting Over

Today started off badly and only got worse. Everyone in my family woke up late this morning. I had only 15 minutes to get ready and catch the bus. I dressed as fast as I could, grabbed an apple and my backpack, and raced to get to the bus stop on time. Fortunately, I just made it. Unfortunately, the bus was pulling away when several kids pointed out that I had on two different shoes. At that moment, I wanted to start the day over.

Pages 24

Sentences and topics will vary.

Page 25

Topic sentences will vary.

Page 26

Topic sentences will vary.

Page 27

Topic sentence: Tony Hawk is an extraordinary skateboarder.

Supporting sentences: He turned professional when he was only 14 years old. Now in his thirties, Tony has won more skateboarding contests than anyone else has. He even made history in 1999 by landing a trick called the "900" at the Summer X Games.

Closing sentence: Tony Hawk may just be the greatest skateboarder in the world.

Paragraphs will vary.

Page 28

Topic sentence: Yesterday our science class went on a field trip to a pond.

Unrelated supporting sentences: Next month we're going to the ocean. That will be fun. One of the boys accidentally fell in. He was really embarrassed.

Page 29

Supporting sentences will vary.

Page 30

Paragraphs will vary.

Page 31

1. O; 2. F; 3. F; 4. O; 5. F; 6. O; Fact and opinion sentences will vary.

Page 32

Paragraphs will vary.

Page 33

Responses and paragraphs will vary.

Page 34

Responses will vary.

Page 35

1. Max had forgotten to check the pot of stew heating up on the stove. 2. Effects: the stew boiled over; the bottom of the pot was scorched; smoke filled the kitchen; dinner was ruined; and Max was in trouble; Paragraphs will vary.

Page 36

Paragraphs will vary.

Page 37

Overused words in paragraph: good, nice, little, big, bad, hard, afraid, sad; Synonyms will vary.

Page 38

Verbs: 1. went; 2. ran; 3. blew; 4. cleaned; 5. laughed; 6. ate; 7. liked; 8. slept; 9. looked; Synonyms will vary. Exact verbs and sentences will vary.

Page 39

Responses will vary.

Page 40

Responses will vary.

Page 41

Responses will vary.

Page 42

Responses will vary.

Page 43

Responses will vary, but all should include commas and quotation marks around the direct words of speakers.

Pages 44–45

1. Chester Greenwood; 2. 3; 3. Who was Chester Greenwood? 4. 5; Outlines will vary.

Page 46

Responses will vary.